The Humours
of Haiku

Edited by
David Cobb

First published 2012 by IRON Press
5 Marden Terrace, Cullercoats
North Shields NE30 4PD
tel/fax +44 (0)191 2531901
ironpress@blueyonder.co.uk
www.ironpress.co.uk

ISBN 978-0-9565725-4-7
Printed by Fieldprint Ltd
Boldon Colliery

IRON Press Books are distributed by Central Books
and represented by Inpress Books Ltd
Collingwood Buildings, 38 Collingwood Street
Newcastle on Tyne NE1 1JF
Tel: 44 (0)191 229 9555
www.inpressbooks.co.uk

contents

Foreword 4
First Monday 10
First Tuesday 12
First Wednesday 14
First Thursday 16
First Friday 18
First Saturday 20
First Sunday 22
Second Monday 24
Second Tuesday 26
Second Wednesday 28
Second Thursday 30
Second Friday 32
Second Saturday 34
Second Sunday 36
Third Monday 38
Third Tuesday 40
Third Wednesday 42
Third Thursday 44
Third Friday 46
Third Saturday 48
Third Sunday 50
Fourth Monday 52
Fourth Tuesday 54
Fourth Wednesday 56
Fourth Thursday 58
Fourth Friday 60
Fourth Saturday 62
Fourth Sunday 64
Fifth Monday 66
Fifth Tuesday 68

Foreword

HAIKU. SMALL EPIPHANIES. SNAPSHOTS OF THE QUOTIDIAN taken from unexpected angles, perhaps with a startling depth of focus. The tiniest of elegies. Breaths of emotion, some light, some dark.

A particular aspect

People appreciate haiku for the concise and lively way poets describe moments in their lives. Careful selection of a limited amount of detail may help readers to connect the poet's experience with their own. Thus a haiku may provide food for anything from idle reflection up to meditation as a life-enhancing practice. There is delight in the imagery the haiku poet uses, whether something everyone is more or less familiar with, or something quite unusual, perhaps exotic. As readers' appreciation of haiku increases they realise images yield more than their plain meanings: they also enrich the haiku with emotional colour. When you sift through these pages we'd like you to be particularly alert to moods and emotions. To the 'humours of haiku', as our title puts it — we use 'humours' in the broader sense of states of mind.

The Humours of Haiku, let's be clear about this, doesn't mean you are supposed to find every haiku in this anthology funny. Far from it. Some will indeed make you want to laugh as they conjure up an incongruous picture, or they may force a smile because they are whimsical or ironic. But there are just as many, if not more, that will bring tears to your eyes, perhaps overwhelm you, leave you gasping. Some may even conjure moods you'd rather not share.

The aim is to explore the range of emotions we can find hints of, a spectrum possibly wider than readers will until now have associated with haiku.

Previous anthologies

In the past two decades quite a few anthologies of English-language haiku have been published in Britain, North America and other countries where English is widely spoken. Some have been arranged by author.[1] Others have been organised within some kind of physical framework — the seasons of the year [2]; a particular environment, such as seaside or urban landscape [3]; a variety of flora or fauna e.g. birds [4]. Anthologies of the second, third and fourth types may have lent credence to the stereotype of haiku as being a 'poetry of Nature'.

There is some truth in that stereotype, but it is far from the whole story. Many haiku are celebrations of Nature, descriptive of some reality, conveying feelings of respect, awe and wonder. But many other haiku rely on interplay between the whole natural world and human nature which is a small part of it. There are also many haiku that are wholly within the human world, dealing with human affairs, behaviour and emotions [5]. Until now the only anthologies put together using human emotions as the criterion have been collections of 'love haiku'. We shall leave it to you to deal with the ambiguities of the selected haiku to decide what 'emotional pigeon holes' they may fit into.

Ambiguity that invites different readings of possible emotion

If you draw up a list of human states of mind — anger, anxiety, gratitude, greed, generosity, pride, and so on — and then try to find examples of them, you will soon run into problems, with the same haiku seeming to fit in more than one pigeon hole. This is because haiku poets draw back from explicit statements, preferring to leave things open-ended, even making deliberate use of ambiguity. You might well glean both a lighter and a darker interpretation of the same haiku.

Let us consider, for example, this haiku by Kohjin Sakamoto, to be found on page 12.

> *his breath*
> *white in the fog*
> *first day of the journey*

There is nothing to pin down how the writer actually felt on that occasion, yet we sense that some quite strong feeling is tucked away there. Can we gain access to it? There are clues in the situation and the imagery — yet at the same time nothing is hard and fast.
Sakamoto's third line might suggest anticipation, but what sort of anticipation? Was he looking forward to reaching a destination, or was he apprehensive about

something? His choice of the image 'fog' might suggest unease about something unknown that lies ahead. His own white breath is mingling with that fog — perhaps he is fearful of getting lost? A lot may depend on our own personal attitude to the colour 'white'. In some cultures it is the prescribed colour for mourners.

And here is another, highly ambiguous haiku to consider. It is by Yoko Ogino. You will find it on page 49.

> hot bath water
> cold on the breastless side
> spring thunder

The ambiguity is caused by the second line, what haikuists sometimes term a 'hinge line'. That is, we can read it both as an extension of line 1 —it is the hot bath water that feels cold, or rather, can't be felt at all. Or we can read line 2 together with line 3, meaning it is the spring thunder she can't feel because of her mastectomy. Rationally, we might conclude that both meanings apply, and that she can feel neither the hot water nor the thunder. But what conclusion might we come to about the poet's emotion? Is it a sorrowful, self-pitying, negative poem about loss? It could be interpreted that way, but it is not the way I understand it. I do have the advantage of knowing that Yoko published an earlier version where the final line was 'another fine day'. That convinces me she means this as a positive, philosophical poem; she is not seeking pity, but telling us that spring is spring, a woman can feel its fever even if she has lost a breast. The reader will surely feel sympathy for the poet

in her misfortune, but also feel immensely strengthened
by her affirmation of life in this bitter-sweet poem.

Sets and headings

We have put the haiku into sets of 8 — thirty sets
in all — according to some inconclusive perception
that the eight haiku in it might, just might, have some
undercurrent of similar emotion. And we shall leave it to
you, the reader, to decide if all 8 haiku in a set actually
share a common current of feeling. The sets needed to
be identified in some way, but the headings should not
steer the reader towards any common denominators of
emotion that the editor might have had in mind. The
use of headings running in serried fashion from *First
Monday* through to *Fifth Tuesday* might seem eccentric,
but it may also serve as a useful reminder that haiku
are best taken in small doses. Eight a day will do more
than keep the doctor away. It will allow plenty of time
for absorption and reflection. So, with thirty sets, there
is enough here to keep you busy for a month. Exceed the
dose and you risk chronic haiku freakitis!

David Cobb
Autumn 2012

[1] e.g. *The IRON Book of British Haiku,* ed. David Cobb and Martin Lucas, IRON Press, 1998

[2] e.g. *Haiku,* ed. David Cobb, British Museum Press, 2002

[3] e.g. *Spindrift – Haiku from the Saxon Shore,* BHS, 1997

[4] e.g. *Wingbeats – British Birds in Haiku,* ed. John Barlow and Matthew Paul, Snapshot Press, 2008

[5] The majority of journals and webzines from which the haiku in this anthology were culled do not follow the much too loose description, that any three-liner 'primarily concerned with human nature' should be regarded as a *senryu*. Those who adopt that definition will regard many of the poems in this anthology as senryu. We can ease our consciences by using the riddling definition the Japanese are said to be comfortable with: if a haiku poet writes a senryu, it's a haiku; and if a senryu poet writes a haiku, it's a senryu. In the West, however, we do not distinguish between haiku and senryu masters. Nowadays Japanese appear to distinguish haiku from senryu mainly on the basis of form (senryu poets are not bound to use either season words or cutting words as haiku poets may be expected to do.) Another distinction may be said to remain: haiku poets involve themselves in the emotions felt by their subjects; whereas senryu poets stand more to one side, perhaps thinking to themselves, 'There but for the grace of God go I!'

Mixed Emotions

Oh !! my beautiful
Three-line haiku ;
Now count the syllab.

four years old
she laughs at the concept
of a hover-fly

Anne-Marie Glasheen

crossing the road
and still on both sides
the reticulated python

Karen Hoy

tied to the rail
of a five-barred gate
coloured bras

Patricia Prime

behind the print
of Hokusai's wave
a damp patch

Jon Baldwin

chicken pox —
she draws red spots
on dolly's tummy

Ron Woollard

early morning rain —
a man tells a boy
about insurance

Hamish Ironside

spring sun
the jolly urologist
mimes vasectomy

Matthew Paul

community cop a bottle of pop in his holster

Fred Schofield

sepia morning
a bicycle spoke
shines firework green

Haf Davies

clear night sky
granny's pin cushion
reflects the moon

Freya Gaea

the way bindweed
coils around purple hebe —
cumulus clouds

Claire Knight

his breath
white in the fog
first day of the journey

Kohjin Sakamoto

first frost —
brimming my hands
a grey mare's breath

Clare McCotter

at the top of the hill
I am still
the same size

Lynne Rees

whistling to myself —
the changing rhythms
of marsh grass

Colin Stewart Jones

how would I see the wind
without the fallen petals

Susan Lee Kerr

FIRST WEDNESDAY

a prisoner's letter
the wide spaces
between words

Jim Kacian

Dead fly —
I was with it
when it died

Ken Jones

Special offer raspberries
I choose the pack
with the moth inside

Maggie West

trampled frost
the horse stands
in its own fog

John Crook

14

nothing but rain
the old pigeon holds out
its other wing

Doreen King

equinox
a family of refugees
feeding the ducks

Matthew Paul

a thrown coin —
the blind accordionist
affects not to hear

Hamish Ironside

fiftieth year —
'bikini line' slips down
my list of things to do

Lynne Rees

ochre sunset over dunes the army watchtower

Clare McCotter

              the howling of wolves
    a lemon falls
        in Palestine

    Keith Coleman

and he too
checks the road is safe to cross
the man in handcuffs

Phillip Murrell

    creaking floors
    beneath the worn rug
    an earthquake zone

    David Cobb

fly struggles in the web —
be thankful for a screaming
we can't hear

John McDonald

guns fall silent
men in opposing dug outs
feel inside their flies

David Cobb

Hiroshima —
I never grumble
about the scorching sun

Yasuhiko Shigemoto

sunlight
fading through stained glass
the laid-up flags

David Cobb

alone in the dunes
sky reflecting
my dog's cataract

Clare McCotter

doctor's office
she tries
to straighten a tulip

Carol Pearce Worthington

colder and colder
a tramp looking for embers
in a pile of ash

Jean-Michel Guillaumond

Don't have the heart
to brush away the cobwebs —
let the wind do it

Bill Wyatt

tin hat
in the exit hole
a blowfly

Ernest J Berry

artificial flowers
grandma puts them in water
to keep them fresh

Klaus-Dieter Wirth

deepening winter
  darkness in the eyes
    of a chained dog

Martin Lucas

stormy moonlight
a small bird roosts in
the scarecrow's pocket

Malcolm Williams

bleak day —
correcting the spelling
         on the beggar's sign

Jackie Hardy

         family picnic
         the new wife's rump
         bigger than mine

         Roberta Beary

daughter-in-law
checking the sell-by dates
in our larder

David Steele

         parenting class —
         my attention wanders
         to distant thunder

         Hamish Ironside

you, moon, behave!
I drive this winding road, you're
bounding left and right

Susan Lee Kerr

one year on —
no tan lines
on my ring finger

Alison Williams

vigilante movie
my elbow
heavy on your knee

Alan Summers

elections again
this time barked at
by a blind dog

David Cobb

Michaelmas
the bus queue flinches
from a butterfly

Matthew Paul

daily newspaper
reading the articles
I agree with

David Bingham

blood test
the old nurse smiles
at my old jokes

John Barlow

whistling kettle —
one more rejection slip
missing the bin

John Kinory

sweltering heat
shouting *the same to you*
to a crow

Beverley George

winter mist
four gravediggers watch
a fifth dig

John Barlow

in the dark
striking the wrong end
of the match

Martin Lucas

not knowing what to do
with his belly button fluff
I put it back

Karen Hoy

out to dinner
ordering garlic sauce
when he does

Marleen Hulst

at the end of Lent the taste of you

Jim Kacian

souvenir T-shirt —
her breasts recommend
the mountain resort

Max Verhart

gathering grassheads —
the Velcro on your
sexy sandals

Graham High

signing his book
for the pretty girl
he mis-spells his name

Cor van den Heuvel

Indian summer
a turtle on a turtle
on a rock

Peggy Willis Lyles

snowfall
his fingers slowly
unbutton me

Roberta Beary

French waitress
my wife refocuses
my attention

John Crook

on the cliff path
a man with a smile ready
in case he knows me

Kate Hall

changing my mind
halfway into
the tattoo

Jörgen Johansson

ice on the window
with my finger I trace your name
and cross it off

Doreen King

before we begin
I ask the therapist
how she feels

Susan King

falling on black ice
I blush
at my own expletives

David Platt

showing them the safe way
dad uses up
all of the sparklers

David Rollins

his side of it,
her side of it.
winter silence

Lee Gurga

breakfast in silence
 wasps circle
the fine cut marmalade

Helen Buckingham

against the standing stone
the sheep's
incurable itch

Mark Rutter

poppy seeds
on the pale chopping board
— period pains

Maeve O'Sullivan

wedding reception
the first course
shark's fin soup

David Cobb

nearly Christmas
I change the loo freshener
from lemon to pine

Doreen King

the print
on the optometrist's business card
suspiciously small

Mykel Board

the deaf man
having trouble
lip reading
my accent

Basem Farid

lonesome scarecrow
one of us trips
the other up

David Cobb

I tell him I'm alone
the look of horror
on the gondolier's face

Maeve O'Sullivan

stark naked ...
bring me more and more
of the sky

Toshi Miyazaki

is it the next stop?
his affirmative causes her
to paint her lips mauve

Colin Blundell

on my way to the dentist's
the sound of a pick-axe
striking stone

Martin Lucas

by the salmon jump
she remembers
her own birth pangs

Ron Woollard

new girl friend
I retouch a self-portrait
with fresh paint

Graham High

Four-one to Germany —
only the shirt swapping
can lift me

Claire Bugler Hewitt

but what of it
that she lied again —
scent of lilies

Dorota Pyra

days off
I see the world
through my toes

Colin Stewart Jones

derelict airfield
forget-me-nots in
the cracked concrete

Malcolm Williams

Mahler has taught me
so much about Resurrection
I take an egg
& hold it
in my hand

A A Marcoff

This rock has waited
a trillion years for me
to stub my toe

Michael Bangerter

with each mile
nearer home, my accent
getting thicker

Colin Maxwell-Charters

a butterfly appears
when there seems to be no hope
to speak of

A A Marcoff

condensation
I draw myself
a happy face

Lynne Rees

after the interview
walking uphill into
the sting of hail

Martin Lucas

the one-man-band man
asks if anybody else
might fancy a go

Colin Blundell

Yes, I say
to the blowsy yellow tulip,
        yes, oh yes ...

David Cobb

                an open-air bath
                sharing it
                with apricot petals

                Yoko Ogino

rainbows of silence
I feel
the colours of things

A A Marcoff

                snowing
                through the blizzard
                particles of me

                Alan Summers

a sharp frost
the nip of the blackbird's beak
taking a raisin

Margery Newlove

sing, little bird, sing —
help us find
a name for the baby

Gilles Fabre

the shape of their sweep
the sweep of their shape
discarded brooms

Michael Fessler

velveting the derelict roof a patch of moon

Clare McCotter

one smooth pebble
falls against another
spring thaw

Greg Piko

deep down in her bag
she says she has an apple
the other man's wife

David Cobb

red light district
a sparrow collects
nest material

Max Verhart

seagulls circling
the London Eye —
our eyes connect

Ron Woollard

new moon
the shadow
in your navel

Mark Rutter

asking directions
of two women in kimono
though I know the way

Michael Fessler

motion of the wave —
applying her lip salve
in the rocking boat

Graham High

spring afternoon
her buttocks peek out
from my shirt

Colin Stewart Jones

travelling alone
I read Turgenev
with you as hero

Frances High

Valentine's Day
my wife reads up
on Henry VIII

Alan Summers

my letter to you
I rejoin the perforations
of two stamps

Graham High

night silence ...
beneath her head
my pins and needles

John Barlow

dancing
over crazy paving
mating butterflies

David Brady

watching you get up
I slide into the warm space
that you leave behind

Andrew Shimield

your pretty knickers
I notice only now
in the washing bowl

Graham High

an old hand puppet
I'm given new licence
to caress your hair

Graham High

one year married
the way the sea
unscrolls up the beach

Doreen King

white camellias —
a whole year since I wrote
a poem for you

Christopher A White

you are now
an enormous hailstone
so I hug you

Toshinori Tsuboichi

love again
caressing her body
avoiding the scar

Basem Farid

Raining —
what a cute small mouth
a tulip has!

Yasuhiko Shigemoto

sultry dusk
on the veranda
    the erotic
    rocking chair

David Cobb

half our life
asleep together
dreaming apart

John Parsons

picking petals
she loves him
enough to cheat

Ron Woollard

planning the trip —
the gentle rolling
of my tongue

Jim Kacian

reaching the road
almost dark almost starless
hooves striking flint

David Platt

slow ships —
among cold shadows my quest
for the face of water

Dejan Bogojevic

a blue field of flax
somewhere there must be boats
to sail on it

David Cobb

departure day
the car covered
with pollen

Dietmar Tauchner

first snow
she runs to every window
just to check

Ron Woollard

December morning
hope fading with each twist
of the car key

Phillip Murrell

train cancellation
an apple
nibbled down to its pips

Phillip Murrell

the firefly in her jar —
nothing she does
makes it light up

Gary Hotham

Christmas week —
the fishmonger's face
expressionless

John Barlow

fluking a red
in the middle pocket —
his deadpan face

Matthew Paul

the drought ended
finding his note
in my raincoat pocket

Carrie Etter

Dangling from her rear view
the clack! clack!
of her wooden crucifix

Ken Jones

from the dark
behind the bag stall
a dirty laugh

Fred Schofield

autumn morning —
a tramp brushes leaves
off the park bench

John Barlow

at the waterfront
a pipe smoker gives the moon
a second look

FrancIs Attard

parents' divorce —
the rip of a page
from the calendar

Dorota Pyra

news of his death
I pluck a rotten tomato
from the vine

Kathy Lippard Cobb

pale light on the Chapel Field
good morning, says Dai,
to gas the moles

Ken Jones

after they've gone
squeezing the toothpaste tube
back into shape

Phillip Murrell

first day of term
six weeks of mould
in the coffee cup

Andrew Detheridge

small art exhibition
the man who farted
follows us

Duro Jaiye

community meeting
the priest adds up
his mileage claims

Matt Morden

the young feminist
adding a bra
to the snowperson

David Rollins

car door clunk
a shell of fresh snow
falls utterly away

Scott Mason

no more than
half itself
the magpie in snow

David Cobb

estuary fog
a bell boomerangs
from shore to shore

Malcolm Williams

under the carpet
the missing piece of the jigsaw
now at the charity shop

Basem Farid

hot bath water
cold on the breastless side
spring thunder

Yoko Ogino

after you leave
your space taken
by light and shade

Frank Williams

All Hallows Eve
a phantom pain
in the missing breast

Doris Heitmeyer

in silence now I cut paper
with my dead mother's
dress-making scissors

Colin Blundell

frozen into
the surface of the pond —
a pair of gloves

David Bingham

our pram
in the charity shop —
you touch the handle

Claire Bugler Hewitt

this photo
of people standing still
by standing stones

David Steele

'odds and sods' drawer
our wedding cake horseshoe
at the very back

Susan King

dinner for one
a gentian collapses
on itself

Doreen King

snow-laden lane —
the muffled horse pulls
an empty cart

Malcolm Williams

open window
a tear is about to jump
from the top floor

Ginka Biliarska

trimming the hedge
still that dent the swing made
forty years ago

Ron Woollard

deep in the cave
I turn off my light and listen
to the darkness

Mark Gilbert

A night of snow — now
even the dustbin
is a work of art

Michael Bangerter

I cut
the lawn — I change
the world

Leo Lavery

supper alone
sounds of the things
I touch

Dorota Pyra

Chopin sonata —
a ripple of moss
across the roof tiles

Diana Webb

the sun setting ...
along the undertaker's roof
a band of blue light

Frank Williams

pink envelopes
even the postman knows
it's a girl

Jon Baldwin

not yet light
a solitary figure walks
between the flying flags

Margery Newlove

mouse tracks
across the frozen lard
in the frying pan

Alan Spence

the polite waiter
under his white sleeve
a snake tattoo

Andrew Shimield

potato-picking
the farmhand's
glittering arc of piss

John McDonald

Sunk gasometer
its curving lattice
cutting through a crimson sky

Ken Jones

a rock
in the middle of nowhere
making it somewhere

Graham High

On holiday —
staring at the ballast
in an empty barge

Ken Jones

the scarecrow's crucified arms hungry for some dark star

Clare McCotter

still lake: a fish jumps
again, again I'm looking
the other way

Susan Lee Kerr

night heat
wherever I go
my pulse

Christopher A White

from the sky's darkness
to the river's darkness
a weeping willow

Dorota Pyra

brought here
to study old ruins
I stroke a cat

Colin Blundell

Easter Sunday
ringing round to hear
who's died lately

Leo Lavery

now what is my shadow
doing out there,
alone in the cold?

Ginka Biliarska

closing-out auction —
the farmer clenches the muscles
in his cheeks

Lee Gurga

dining out alone —
the waiter seats me
right by the door

Frank Williams

mist across the bay
between our words
the waves ... the waves

Ion Codrescu

beside the waterfall
the timeless reverie
soon exhausted

Graham High

wee hours
looking for someone to talk to
in cyberspace

Yoko Ogino

New Year's Day —
yards from the pub
a frozen half in a pint glass

Frank Williams

bog cotton
in the breeze — the whistler
strives for a tune

Fred Schofield

watching Wednesday lose again
with an old friend —
the floodlit rain

Ian Storr

mud pack
watching her young face
harden

Helen Buckingham

quiet afternoon
all my ambitions buried
in a foot of snow

Lee Gurga

First day of the year —
one ring of the telephone
followed by silence

David Burleigh

again and again
the crow tries to carry
three nuts

Margery Newlove

buffet tea:
I take a plate
too small for my greed

Helen Robinson

walking in the snow
for no other reason than
no one else has yet

Andrew Detheridge

not out overnight
he sticks his chewing gum
to the bat handle

André Surridge

a brisk wind —
a pigeon puts its foot
on a slice of bread

Frank Williams

angling for flat fish —
as big as your palm
or a double bed?

Hisashi Miyazaki

half moon —
a sudden craving
for water melon

Max Verhart

Earthrise
not ours
to see

Helen Buckingham

my best friend died —
some tiny grains of dust
on our chessboard

Robert Bebek

up in the attic
the smile
of a dusty clown

Ruth Franke

scattering ashes
the odd places he fancied
fairgrounds and wells

David Cobb

day after his death
the need for his hat to go
into the cupboard

David Steele

midway through the lament
opening my eyes
to see hers closed

Maeve O'Sullivan

Anzac Day
a baby's cry fills
our minute's silence

Beverley George

Summer lightning —
At the top of the temple mountain
The boy with the land-mined
Half face.

(Pre Rup, Angkor, 31.8.00)
Tito

a caterpillar
crawls up a cannon barrel —
rain, all's quiet

Luko Paljetak

in his greenhouse
the snooker player
lines up loose tomatoes

Malcolm Williams

art class ...
she starts drawing
the shadow first

K Ramesh

the hand gestures
of a lady giving directions
over the phone

Martin Lucas

working from home
with my best business voice
in my nightie

Karen Hoy

first cricket
I quickly blow-dry
my shampooed hair

Yoko Ogino

casino night
in the croupier's cleavage
her crucifix

Phillip Murrell

On the washing line
the sun peeping right through it —
a hole in my sock

Bill Wyatt

late summer sunset
at the end of my novel
tears and dancing

Lynne Rees

ninety-two
just congratulations
from the cleaning lady

Ruth Franke

on the marble slab
the flesh of two fish
touching each other

Graham High

Christmas party
the exile sits closest
to the tree

Višjna McMaster

in the hospice
their granny, smiling —
with someone else's teeth

Michael Bangerter

arguing about what to do —
two children
playing mothers and fathers

Doreen King

Mothers' Day ...
my sister brings a plant
bigger than mine

Brian Tasker

hummingbird
I pluck its colours
to create my own state

Alan Summers

wasted again
the bang of the door ...
nobody home

Joanna Ashwell

high technology
I give it a good
thump

Peter Williams

running ... running
catching it at the last moment
the wrong train

Basem Farid

unlabeled photos
both sides of the family
disavowing such kin

Carolyn Hall

Harley Davidson Club
all black leather, glittering chrome
and dentures

Jann Wirtz

'Long May They Reign'
in the coronation mug
false teeth

Ken Jones

Garter Ceremony
the Conqueror of Everest
struggles with the stairs

Jon Iddon

summer fete
the Punch and Judy man
losing his voices

Matthew Paul

'missing' poster
the young woman's face
just like mine

Juliet Wilson

Acknowledgements

Key: BS = Blithe Spirit   ms = unpublished at time of selection

Joanna Ashwell wasted again: BS 11/4 **Francis Attard**
at the waterfront: BS 18/2 **Jon Baldwin** behind the print,
pink envelopes: BS 18/2 **Michael Bangerter** This rock has
waited, *Eyelines,* Kite Modern Poetry Series, 2002; A night of
snow: BS 16/2, in the hospice: BS 15/4 **John Barlow** night
silence, Christmas week, autumn morning: *Waiting for the
Seventh Way,* Snapshot Press, 2006; blood test: *Modern Haiku
38.2, 2007* **Roberta Beary** family picnic, snowfall: *The
Unworn Necklace,* Snapshot Press, 2007 (hardback edn. 2011)
Robert Bebek my best friend died: *Clouds in the Shortest
Night, Planetart,* 2009 **Ernest J Berry** tin hat: *A Korean War
Experience,* 2000 **David Bingham** daily newspaper: BS 18/1,
frozen into: BS 20/1 **Colin Blundell** is it the next stop, in
silence now I cut paper, the one-man-band-man, brought here:
all *On a Barn Ridge Tile,* Hub, 2010 **Mykel Board** the print:
A Face from Another World, Spring Street Haiku Group, 2007
Dejan Bogojevic slow ships: *My Quest for the Face of Water,*
Apokalipsa, 2008 **David Brady** dancing: BS 10/2 **Helen
Buckingham** breakfast in silence: *Mayfly No 49,* 2010; mud
pack: *Earth,* BHS, 2009; Earthrise: BS 20/1 **Claire Bugler
Hewitt** Four-one to Germany: BS 20/3 our pram: BS 12/3
David Burleigh First day of the year: *Kō,* 24/4, 2010 **David
Cobb** creaking floors, guns fall silent, lonesome scarecrow,
wedding reception, scattering ashes: all ms; elections again:
Whirligig 2/1; yes, I say: *Zen Space,* 2011; deep down in her
bag: BS 13/2; sultry dusk: *Spitting Pips,* Equinox Press, 2009; a
blue field of flax: BS 19/3; no more than: grand prize, Ohi Ocha
International Haiku Contest, 2010; sunlight: *Jumping from
Kiyomizu,* Iron Press, 1996 **Kathy Lippard Cobb** news of
his death: prize winner, AN5 Haiku Contest anthology, 2002
Ion Codrescu mist across the bay: *Waiting in Silence,* 2009
Keith Coleman the howling of wolves: BS 20/3; **John**

Crook trampled frost: BS 10/1; French waitress: BS 10/2
Haf Davies sepia morning: *Light*, BHS, 2006 **Andrew Detheridge** walking in the snow: BS 11/1; first day of term: BS 13/4 **Carrie Etter** the drought ended: BS 12/4 **Gilles Fabre** sing, little bird, sing: *Clouds in the Shortest Night*, 2009 **Basem Farid** the deaf man: BS 13/2, love again: BS 15/2, under the carpet: BS 13/5, running ... running: BS 12/4 **Michael Fessler** the shape of their sweep: BS 16/4, asking directions: BS 16/2 **Ruth Franke** ninety-two, up in the attic: both *Slipping Through Water*, Wiesenburg, 2010 **Freya Gaea** clear night sky: *Light*, BHS, 2006 **Beverley George** sweltering heat: BS 14/4; Anzac Day: BS 16/2 **Anne-Marie Glassheen** four years old: BS 18/2 **Jean-Michel Guillaumond** colder and colder: BS 13/4 **Lee Gurga** his side of it; closing-out auction: *In the Cottonwood Tops*, 2005; quiet afternoon: *A Penny Face Up*, 2000 **Carolyn Hall** back again: BS 14/2; unlabelled photos BS 11/4 **Kate Hall** on the cliff path: BS 12/2 **Jackie Hardy** bleak day: *Counting the Waves, Bloodaxe*, 1998 **Doris Heitmeyer** All Hallows Eve: *Nickels on my Palm*, Spring Street Haiku Group, 2004 **Frances High** travelling alone: BS 16/2 **Graham High** on the marble slab, beside the waterfall: *Once Around the Sun*, Ram, 2004; gathering grassheads, your pretty knickers, an old hand puppet, my letter to you: *A Bigger Ocean*, Ram, 2010; new girl friend: BS 14/3 motion of the waves: BS 12/2 a rock: *Earth*, BHS, 2009 **Gary Hotham** the firefly in her jar: BS 10/3 **Karen Hoy** crossing the road: *River*, BHS, 2005; working from home: BS 12/3; not knowing what to do: *Another Country*, Gomer, 2011 **Marleen Hulst** out to dinner: BS 20/3 **Hamish Ironside** early morning rain, a thrown coin, parenting class: all *Our Sweet Little Time*, IRON Press, 2009 **Jon Iddon** Garter Ceremony: BS 15/2 **Duro Jaiye**

small art exhibit: *Enhaiklopaedia,* Hailstones, 2007 **Jörgen Johansson** changing my mind: *Snowdrops,* 2009 **Ken Jones** Dead fly: BS 20/1, Pale light on the Chapel Field: BS 12/2, Sunk gasometer: BS 16/1, On holiday: BS 15/4 , Long May They Reign: BS 13/2 Dangling from her rear view: BS 18/3 **Jim Kacian** a prisoner's letter, *Snapshots 9;* at the end of Lent the taste of you: *Stir the Hive No. 1,* planning the trip: *Borderlands,* Red Moon Press, 2007; **Susan Lee Kerr** how would I see the wind: BS 16/2; you moon, behave: *Night Bus,* Ram, 2002; still lake: a fish jumps BS 12/4 **Doreen King** nothing but rain, one year married, dinner for one: *Sweep of Light,* Hub, 2008; ice on the window: BS 13/1, nearly Christmas: BS 14/4; arguing about what to do: BS 12/2 **Susan King** before we begin: BS 12/4; 'odds and sods' drawer: BS 13/4 **John Kinory** whistling kettle: BS 15/2 **Claire Knight** the way bindweed: BS 19/3 **Leo Lavery** I cut: BS 17/3, Easter Sunday: BS 12/2 **Martin Lucas** deepening winter, on my way to the dentist's, after the interview, the hand gestures: *Earthjazz,* Ram, 2003; in the dark: BS 12/3 **Peggy Willis Lyles** Indian summer: *Phosphorescence,* Red Moon Press, 2010 **Clare McCotter** first frost BS 19/1; alone in the dunes: *World Haiku Review* 7/2, 2009; ochre sunset: *Presence No. 38,* 2009; velveting the derelict roof: *Shamrock No. 13,* Irish Haiku Society; the scarecrow: ms **John McDonald** fly struggles in the web, potato-picking: *Tuim Tin Tassie,* Hub **Višnja McMaster** Christmas party: BS 14/3 **A A Marcoff** rainbows of silence: *Wild Suns,* Hub; Mahler has taught me: *The Dialectics of Rain,* Hub, 2007; a butterfly appears; BS 13/4 **Scott Mason** car door clunk: BS 18/2 **Colin Maxwell-Charters** with each mile: BS 14/2 **Hisashi Miyazaki** angling for flatfish: *Enhaiklopaedia,* Hailstones **Toshi Miyazaki** stark naked: *Japanese Haiku 2008,* Gendai Haiku Kyokai **Matt Morden** community meeting: *A Dark Afternoon,* Snapshot Press, 2001

Phillip Murrell after they've gone: BS 18/2; casino night BS 15/2; and he too: BS 20/2; December morning: *Flat,* BHS, 2001; train cancellation: BS 20/1 **Margery Newlove** a sharp frost: BS 17/1; not yet light: BS 16/4; again and again: BS 14/4 **Yoko Ogino** an open-air bath, hot bath water, wee hours, first cricket: *Spring Thunder,* Proton, 1999 **Maeve O'Sullivan** poppy seeds: BS 17/1; I tell him I'm alone, midway through the lament: both *Initial Response,* Alba, 2011; **Luko Paljetak** a caterpillar: *Hairdresser for Chrysanthemums,* Apokalipsa, 2008 **John Parsons** half our life: BS 14/3 **Matthew Paul** spring sun: equinox; Michaelmas, summer fete: *The Regulars,* Snapshot Press; fluking a red: BS 15/2 **Greg Piko** one smooth pebble: *River,* BHS, 2005 **David Platt** reaching the road: BS 10/1; falling on black ice: BS 16/2 **Patricia Prime** tied to the rail: BS 18/2 **Dorota Pyra** from the sky's darkness: *Silver Fry Flicker,* international Ghent haiku festival anthology, 2010; parents' divorce, supper alone, but what of it: all ms. **Lynne Rees** at the top of the hill, fiftieth year, condensation, late summer sunset: all ms. **Helen Robinson** buffet tea BS 12/3 **David Rollins** the young feminist: BS 11/1; showing them the safe way: BS 15/4 **Mark Rutter** against the standing stone: BS 16/3; new moon: BS 15/4 **Kohjin Sakamoto** his breath: BS 17/4 **Fred Schofield** community cop; from the dark: *Wet Grass Laughing;* bog cotton: BS 16/2 **Yasuhiko Shigemoto** Hiroshima: BS 14/3 raining: BS 18/2 **Andrew Shimield** watching you get up: BS 11/2; the polite waiter: BS 16/1 **Alan Spence** mouse tracks: *Seasons of the Heart,* Canongate, 2000 **David Steele** daughter-in-law: *Presence* No. 42, 2010; this photo: BS 10/2, day after his death: BS 13/2 **Colin Stewart Jones** whistling to myself, days off, spring afternoon: all ms. **Ian Storr** watching Wednesday lose again: BS 13/4 **Alan Summers** vigilante movie: *Symmetry Pebbles,* 2011; snowing, *Haiku Calendar 2011,* Snapshot Press;

Valentine's Day: BS 20/3; hummingbird: *Haijinx Vol 4, No. 1*, 2011 **André Surridge** not out overnight: *Presence No. 42*, 2010 **Brian Tasker** Mother's Day: BS 10/2 **Dietmar Tauchner** departure day: *The Heron's Nest, Vol. V8*, 2003 **Tito** Summer lightning: BS 11/2 **Toshinori Tsubouchi** you are now: *Japanese Haiku 2008,* Gendai Haiku Kyokai **Cor van den Heuvel** signing his book: *A Face from Another World,* Spring Street Haiku Group, 2007 **Max Verhart** souvenir T-shirt, red light district, half moon: *Only the White,* 't Schrijverke, 2008 **Diana Webb** Chopin sonata: *Presence No. 42*, 2010 **Maggie West** Special offer raspberries: BS 13/2 **Christopher A White** white camellias: BS 20/3; night heat: BS 19/3 **Alison Williams** one year on: BS 17/3 **Frank Williams** after you leave, dining out alone: *Rush Hour Over,* Hub, 2008; the sun setting, a brisk wind: *Faraway Places;* New Year's Day: *Bumping Along,* Hub, 2001 **Malcolm Williams** estuary fog: winner, BHS James W Hackett Award 2008; snow-laden lane BS 19/1; in his greenhouse: BS 17/4; stormy moonlight **Peter Williams** high technology BS 11/4 **Juliet Wilson** 'missing' poster: BS 19/1 **Klaus-Dieter Wirth** artificial flowers: BS 12/4 **Jann Wirtz** Harley Davidson Club: BS 20/2 **Ron Woollard** chicken pox: BS 16/3, by the salmon jump: *River,* BHS, 2005, seagulls circling: *Night Bus,* 2002; picking petals: BS 13/2, first snow: BS 18/1, trimming the hedge: BS 15/4 **Carol Pearce Worthington** doctor's office: *Mayfly No. 49*, 2010 **Bill Wyatt** Don't have the heart: BS 13/4; On the washing line BS 15/4

Every effort has been made to contact copyright holders and to attribute poems correctly. When, on a very few occasions, the attempts were unsuccessful, we chose to print the poems anyway, trusting our instincts that the contributor would rather be in than out. This seems a reasonable course of action when all but one of the poets we approached opted for inclusion. If any defect is noted and information is forwarded to IRON Press we will put it right in any subsequent edition.

David Cobb wishes to record his special thanks to **Lynne Rees** who came with him part of the way on the trail to produce this anthology, but had to retire under pressure of other writing commitments before the final typescript could be established.